I0752994

This Journal Belongs To

____

Date

____

Herbs & Aromatherapy Journal

Herbs and Aromatherapy Journal

Hardback Edition

ISBN: 978-1-7343258-3-6

Published By:
Rebecca at the Well Foundation
https://www.RATW.org

Printed in the United States of America

www.ingramcontent.com/pod-product-compliance
Lightning Source LLC
LaVergne TN
LVHW071629100826
845154LV00005BA/113
* 9 7 8 1 7 3 4 3 2 5 8 3 6 *